INTRODUCTION

Ever since I wrote and published *TEACHING RHYTHM (FOR ALL INSTRUMENTS)* back in the 1960's, I have had numerous requests to write a sequel expanding upon one of the topics in the book — syncopation. This study, while a little late in coming, is a response to those requests.

Many beginner books dealing with reading rhythm contain syncopation exercises to a greater or lesser degree. And since there are only a few elements involved in reading syncopated rhythms, most of these books will demonstrate somewhat similar exercises. What distinguishes this study from other books is the format for the progression of rhythmic exercises, the nature of the exercises themselves, the in-depth presentation of the topic, and the overall design of the book. Moreover, this study presents rhythmic patterns covering 8th and 16th-note syncopation as well as quarter and 8th-note syncopation.

Like my book *TEACHING RHYTHM*, the exercises in this study just involve the reading of rhythm without pitch. While it is essentially a book for drummers, players on all instruments can benefit from its use. For those who are not drummers, simply clap the rhythms or tap them on a table. Melodies could also be improvised based upon the rhythmic patterns in each exercise.

The part of the title which includes the words "AND BEYOND" refers to the final few sections dealing with syncopated accents, sticking patterns that produce syncopated sounds, and rolls on syncopated rhythms.

TABLE OF CONTENTS

PART ONE

PREPARATORY EXERCISES

READING BASIC RHYTHM
WITH WHOLE, 1/2, 1/4 & 1/8 NOTES,
AND THEIR EQUIVALENT RESTS

Learning to read basic notation with whole, half, quarter and eight-notes must first precede learning to read syncopated rhythmic patterns. **PART ONE** presents an extensive array of preparatory exercises with basic rhythms which will pave the way for a smooth transition into reading the quarter and eighth-note syncopated rhythmic patterns presented in **PART TWO**.

Except for a few summary-style pages dealing with hand-foot reading, a bass drum part is omitted. I suggest, however, that the bass is played on every downbeat throughout each exercise.

Dynamic marks are sprinkled sparsely throughout the book. Since the basic aim is to develop skill in reading patterns of syncopated rhythm, I felt it somewhat unnecessary and detracting to include extensive dynamic markings. For additional reading material containing exercises replete with dynamics, I recommend the following books:

MUSICAL STUDIES FOR THE INTERMEDIATE SNARE DRUMMER
RHYTHMIC PATTERNS OF CONTEMPORARY MUSIC
INTERMEDIATE DUETS FOR SNARE DRUM

INTRODUCING 1/4 NOTES, 1/4 RESTS, 1/2 NOTES, 1/2 RESTS, WHOLE NOTES, WHOLE RESTS

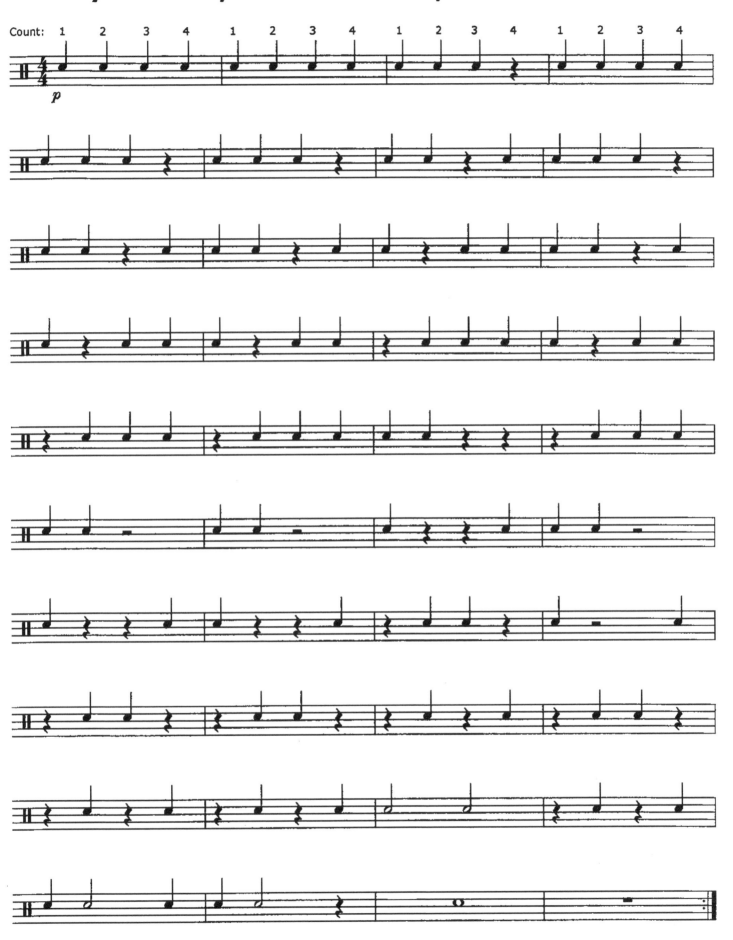

3

INTRODUCING TIES FROM 1/4, 1/2, AND WHOLE NOTES

A tie is a curved line above or below the heads of two notes (of the same pitch) indicating they are to be played for a duration equal to the sum of the two notes. For a drummer, aside from striking a cymbal or rolling on a note, there is no way to sustain the duration of its sound. Simply strike the note on which a tie begins, then count the note on which the tie ends without striking it.

1/4 AND 1/2 NOTES IN 3/4 TIME

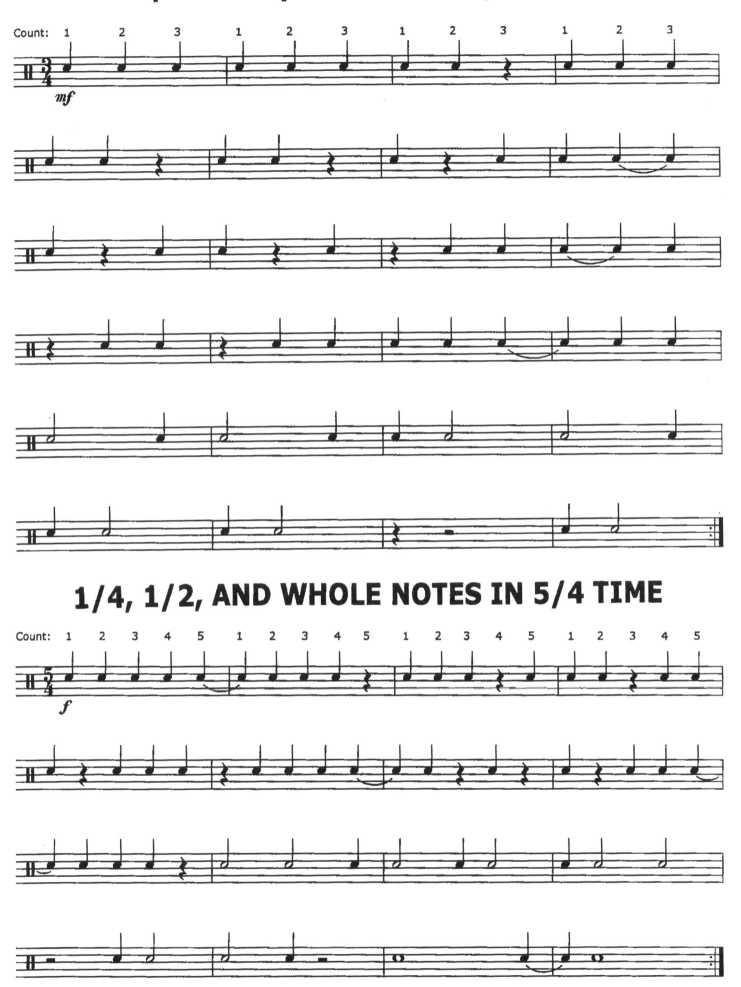

1/4, 1/2, AND WHOLE NOTES IN 5/4 TIME

1/4, 1/2, AND WHOLE NOTES IN SPACE

The following exercise has many rests, leaving a great deal of space between the notes. To play accurately, *be sure to count.*

READING 1/4 AND 1/2 NOTES
WITH THE BASS DRUM INCLUDED

INTRODUCING 1/8 NOTES (♪♪ = ♫)

INTRODUCING 8TH RESTS ON THE UPBEAT (♪ 𝄾)
(In reading 8th notes the upbeat is the count of "an")

9

INTRODUCING 8TH RESTS ON THE DOWNBEAT (𝄾 ♪)

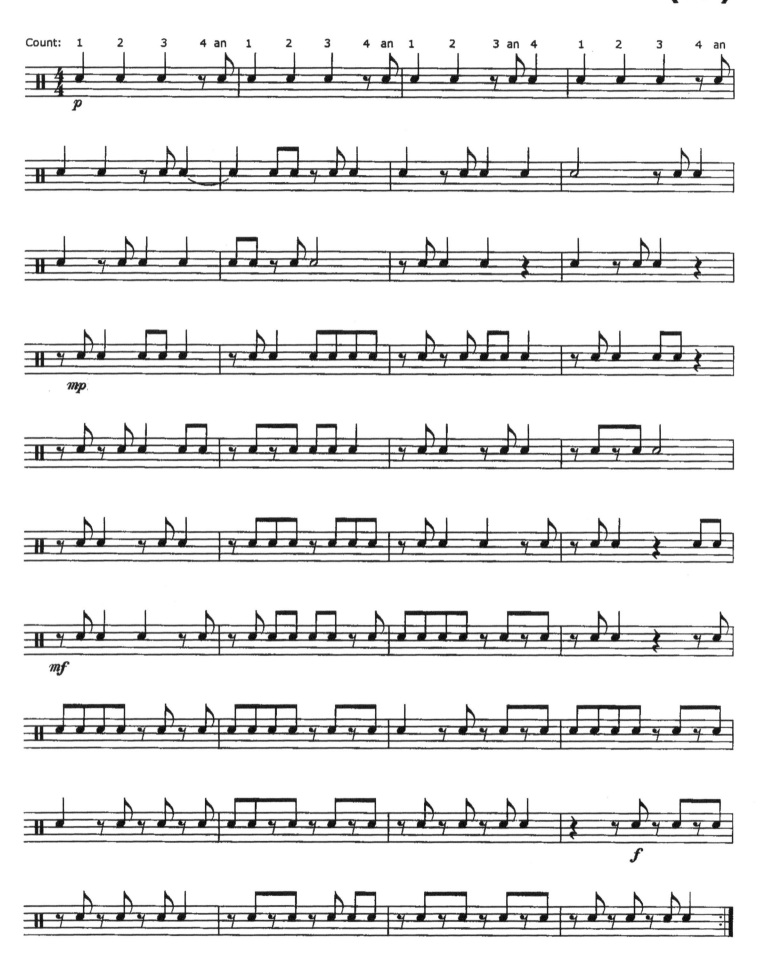

8TH RESTS ON THE UPBEAT AND DOWNBEAT

1/8 AND 1/4 NOTES IN SPACE

Once again, the following exercise presents many rests, leaving a great deal of space between the notes. *BE SURE TO COUNT!*

(fermata)

* A fermata is a pause in the music for an unspecified amount of time. Watch the conductor for an indication of when to continue playing.

TIES TO AND FROM 8TH NOTES

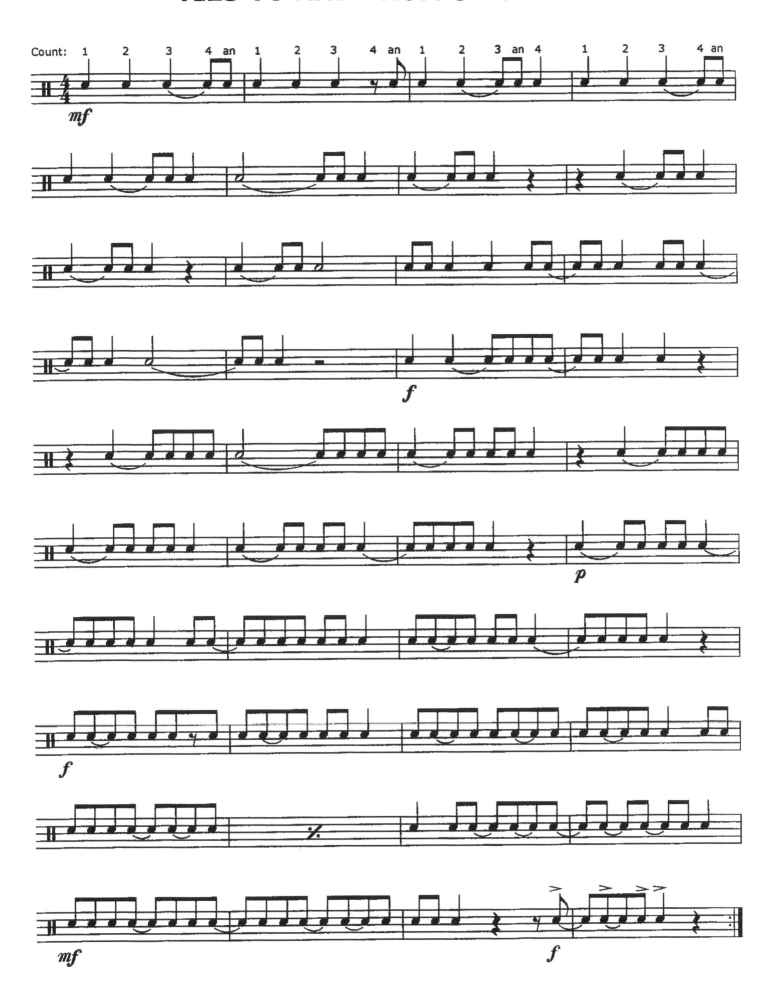

SUMMARY IN 3/4 TIME

SUMMARY IN 5/4 TIME

READING 1/8 AND 1/4 NOTES
WITH THE BASS DRUM AND FLAMS INCLUDED

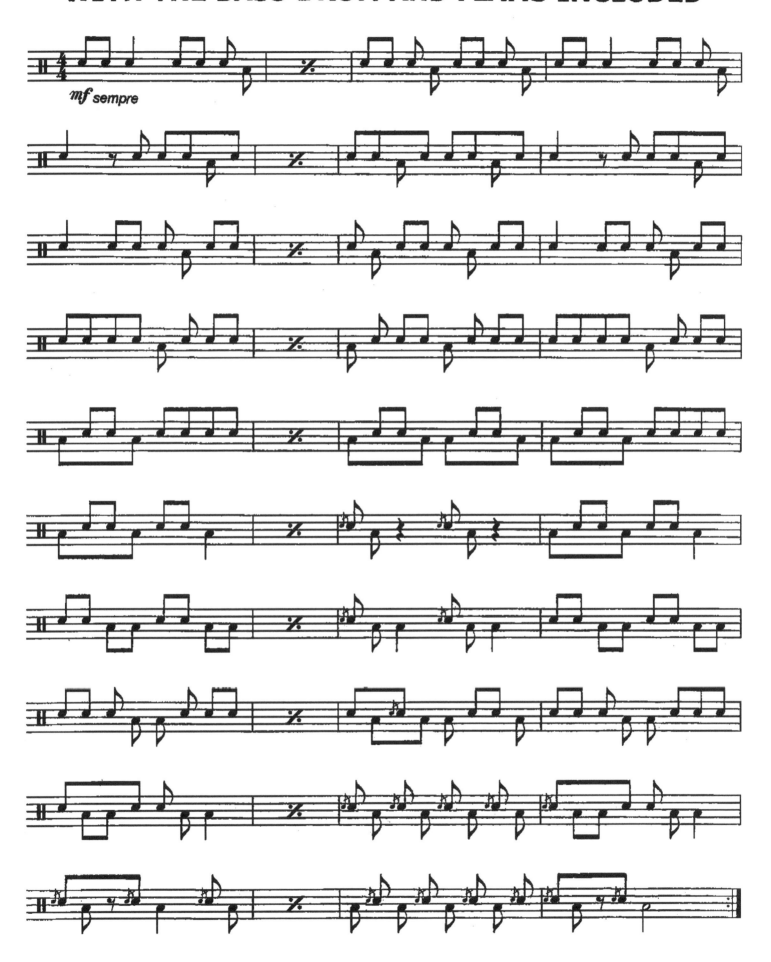

INTRODUCING A DOT AFTER 1/2 NOTES AND 1/4 NOTES

A dot placed after a note increases its duration by half. A half-note is worth two beats in 4/4 time, so a dotted half-note is worth two beats plus another beat, totalling three beats in all.

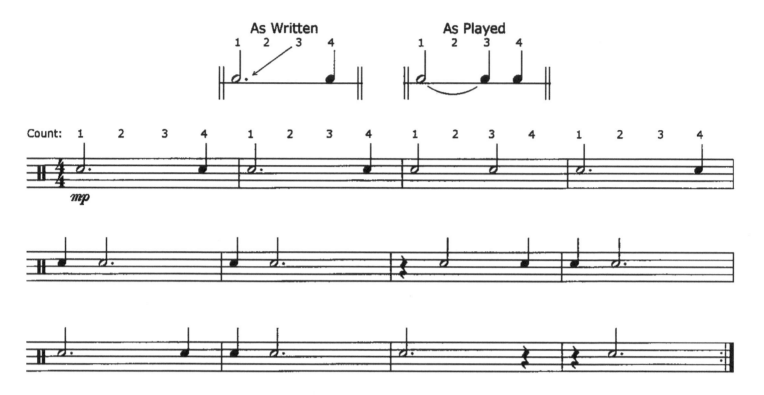

A quarter-note is worth one beat in 4/4 time, so a dot placed after a quarter-note increases its duration to a beat-and-a-half.

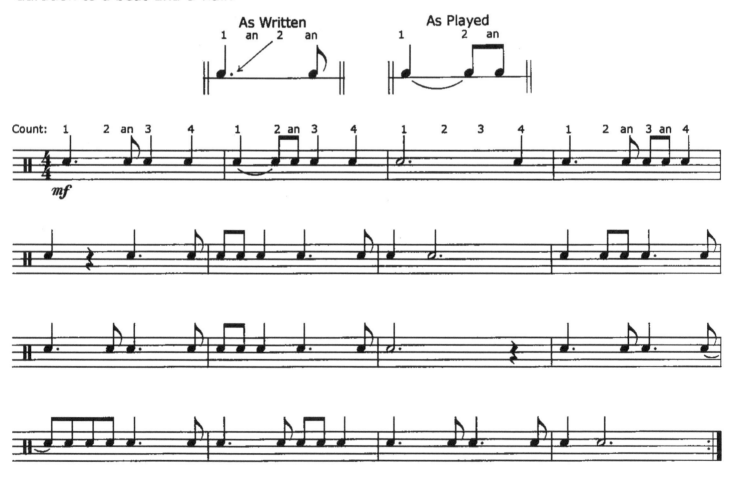

PART TWO

READING SYNCOPATED RHYTHMS WITH 1/4 AND 1/8 NOTES

So just what is syncopation? In 4/4 time the first and third beats are normally stressed. If, instead, the second and fourth beats are stressed, the rhythm may be considered syncopated. The stress can also shift by less than a beat so it falls on an upbeat, in which case the stress is shifted by an eight-note. In other words, upbeats when stressed will produce the sound of syncopated rhythm.

When it comes to actually reading rhythmic notation with quarter and eighth-notes, syncopation involves reading patterns of rhythm with the quarter-note (worth one-full beat in "quarter" time) being played on the upbeat instead of the downbeat.

There are six basic patterns:

From now on the plus sign (+) will be used in place of the word "an," but still count with the word "an" when you see the plus sign above a note.

17

BASIC SYNCOPATED RHYTHMIC PATTERN NUMBER 1

SUMMARY INCLUDING PREVIOUS RHYTHMS

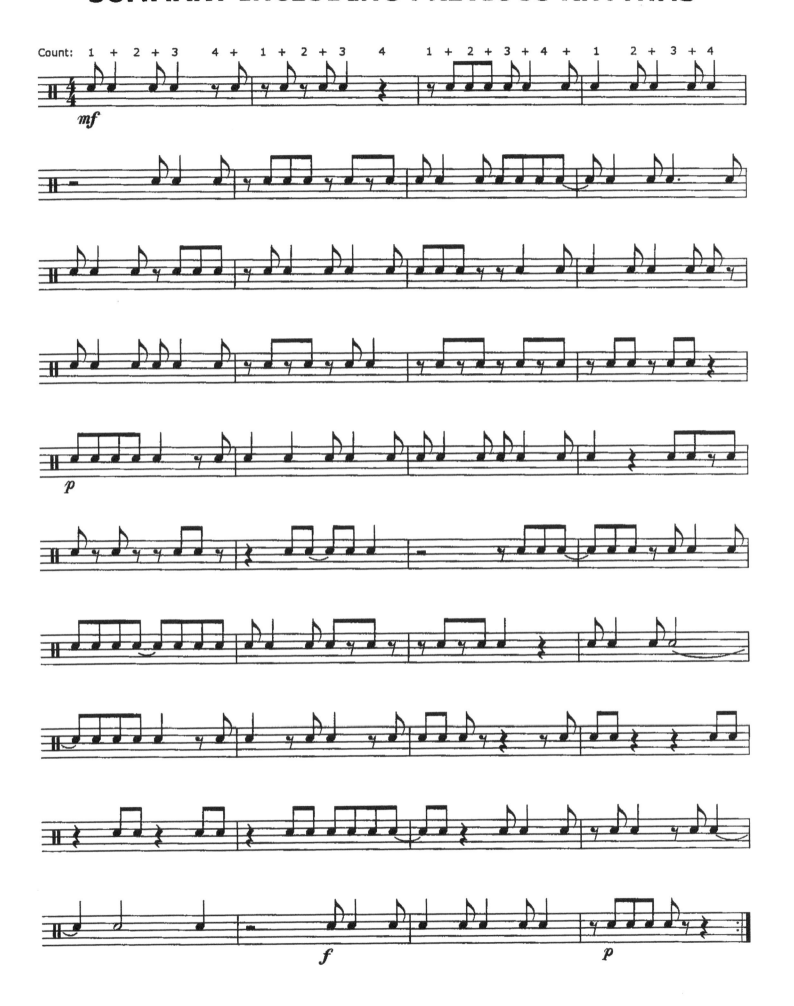

BASIC SYNCOPATED RHYTHMIC PATTERN NUMBER 2

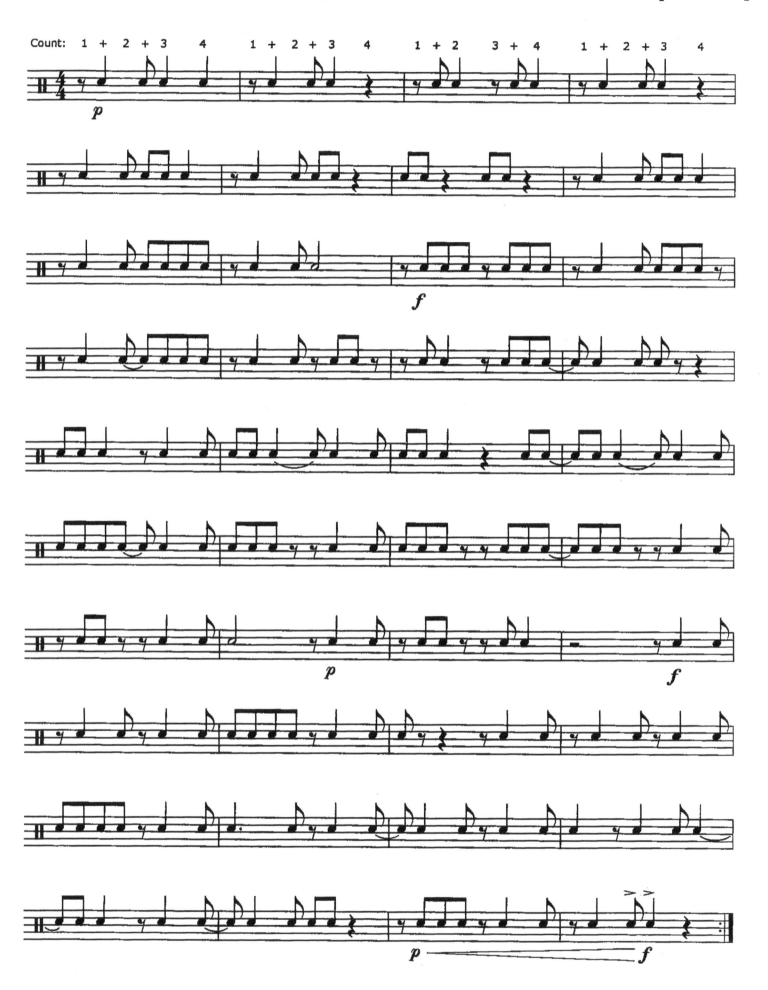

SUMMARY INCLUDING (♪♩ ♪) and (𝄾♩ ♪)

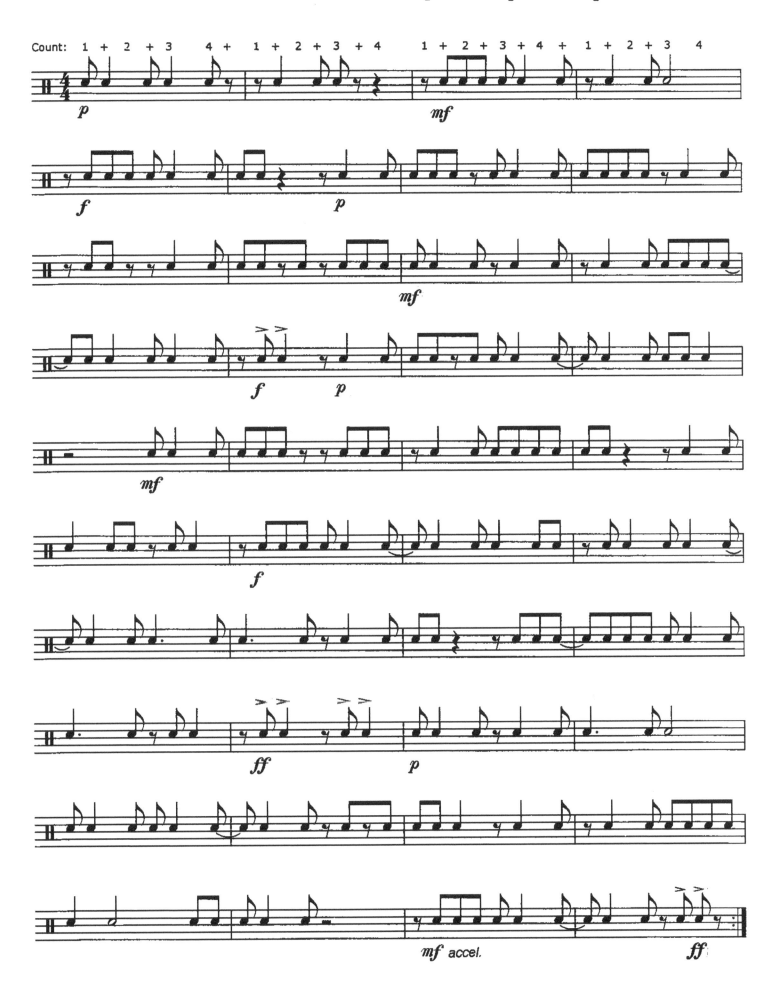

21

BASIC SYNCOPATED RHYTHMIC PATTERNS THREE AND FOUR

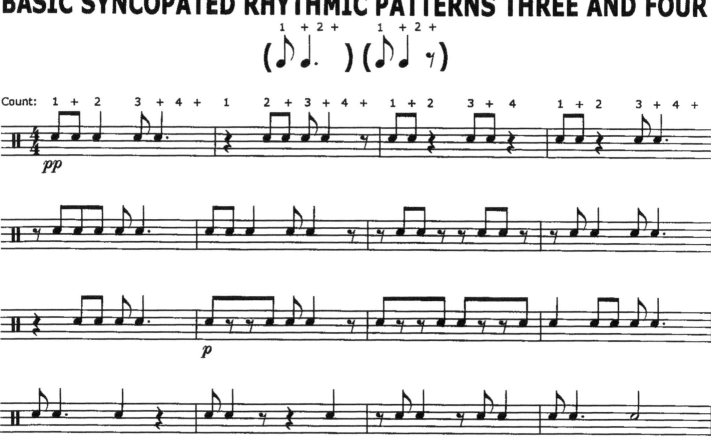

SUMMARY INCLUDING (♪♩ ♪) (♪♩ ♪) (♪♩.) (♪♩ ♪)

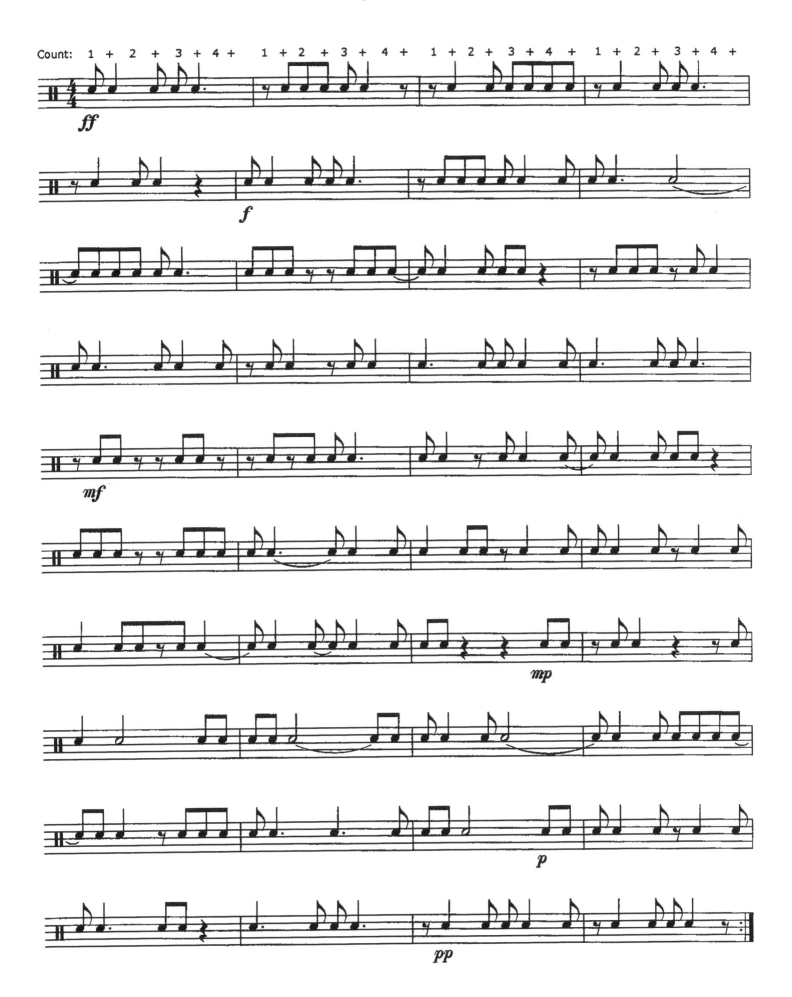

23

BASIC SYNCOPATED RHYTHMIC PATTERNS FIVE AND SIX

SUMMARY INCLUDING

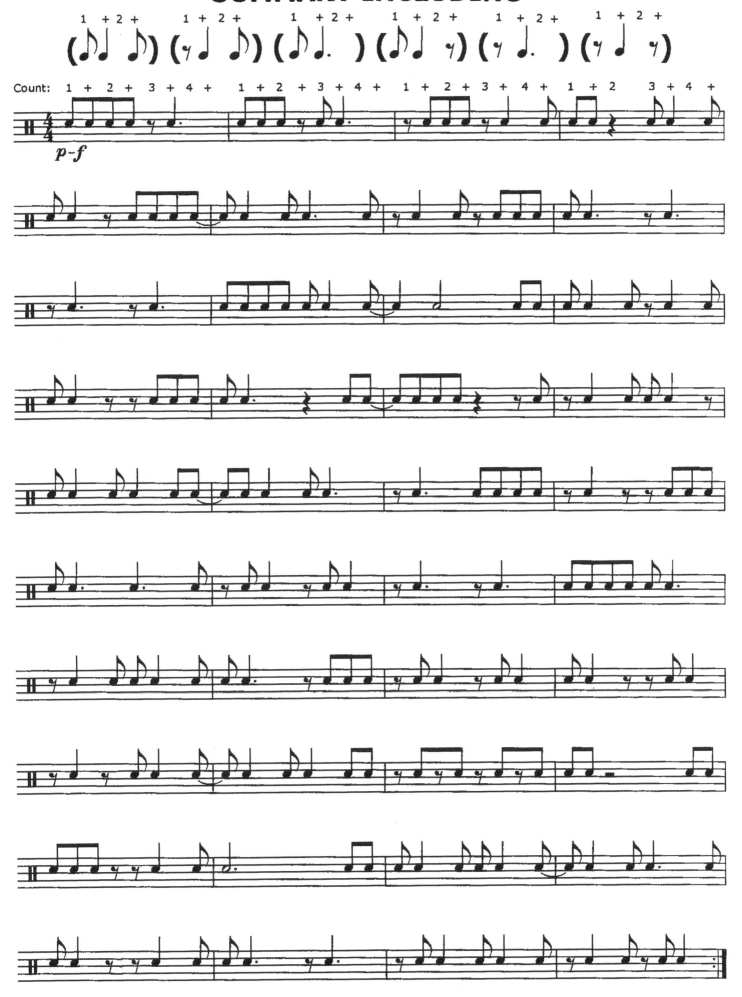

SYNCOPATED RHYTHMIC PATTERNS OVER 3 AND 4 BEATS

READING SYNCOPATED RHYTHMIC PATTERNS IN 3/4 TIME

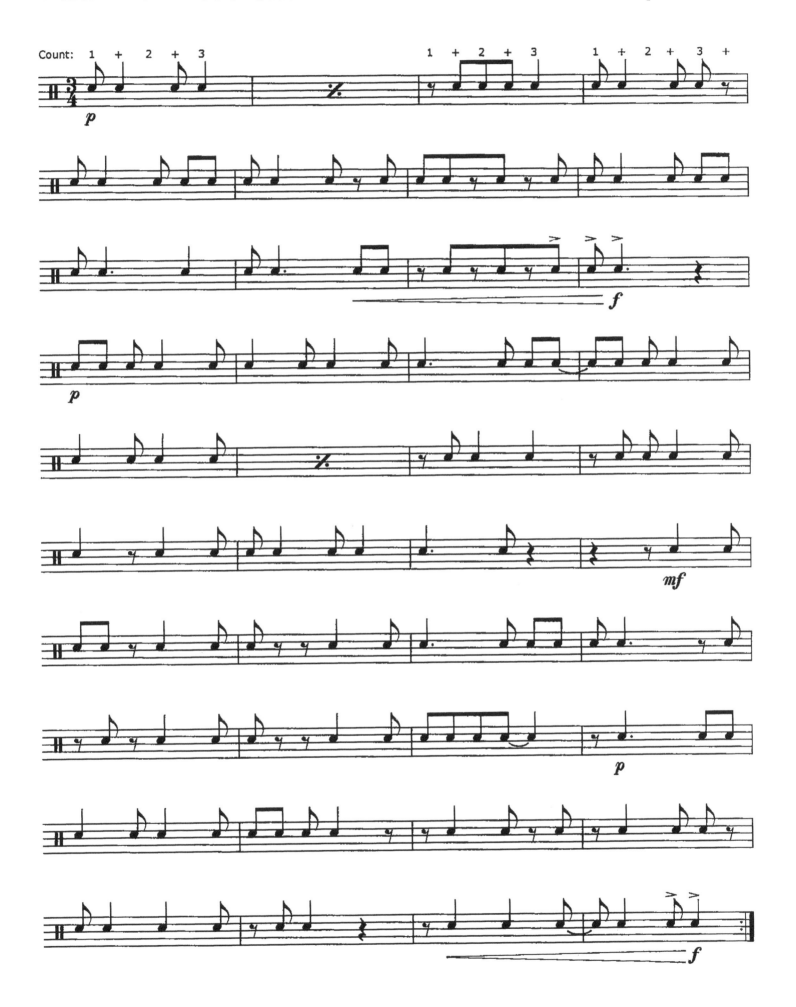

SUMMARY OF SYNCOPATED RHYTHMIC PATTERNS
WITHIN CHANGING TIME SIGNATURES

SYNCOPATION IN SPACE

READING SYNCOPATION
WITH THE BASS DRUM INCLUDED

PART THREE

READING 16TH NOTES
AND 16TH RESTS

Learning to read basic notation with 16th notes and 16th-rests must first precede learning to read syncopated rhythmic patterns with these notes, and this section presents an extensive array of preparatory exercises which will allow for a smooth transition into reading the 16th note syncopation in **PART FOUR.**

Since there are four 16th notes to a beat, a four-syllable count is necessary to reflect the position of each 16th note within that beat. There are several different counts that can be used, but the one I suggest is:

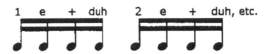

However, in order to keep the count as clear as possible, and the pages free of congestion, I have indicated the "duh" part of the count with just the letter "d," but say "duh," not "d."

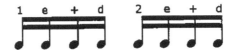

Different teachers may use other counts that are just as good, but whatever count you use, the important thing is that you *do* count throughout the reading of each exercise.

INTRODUCING 16TH NOTES (♪♪♪♪ = ♬♬)

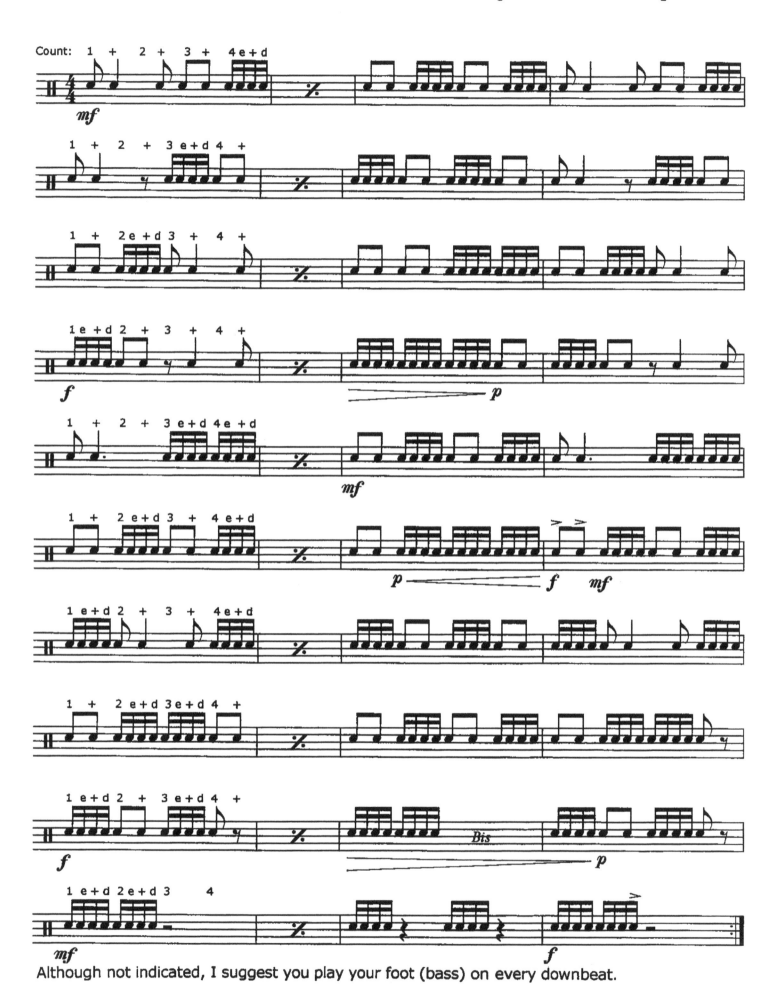

Although not indicated, I suggest you play your foot (bass) on every downbeat.

16TH NOTES COMBINED WITH 8TH NOTES

16TH NOTES COMBINED WITH 8TH NOTES (♫♩)

READING COMBINATIONS OF

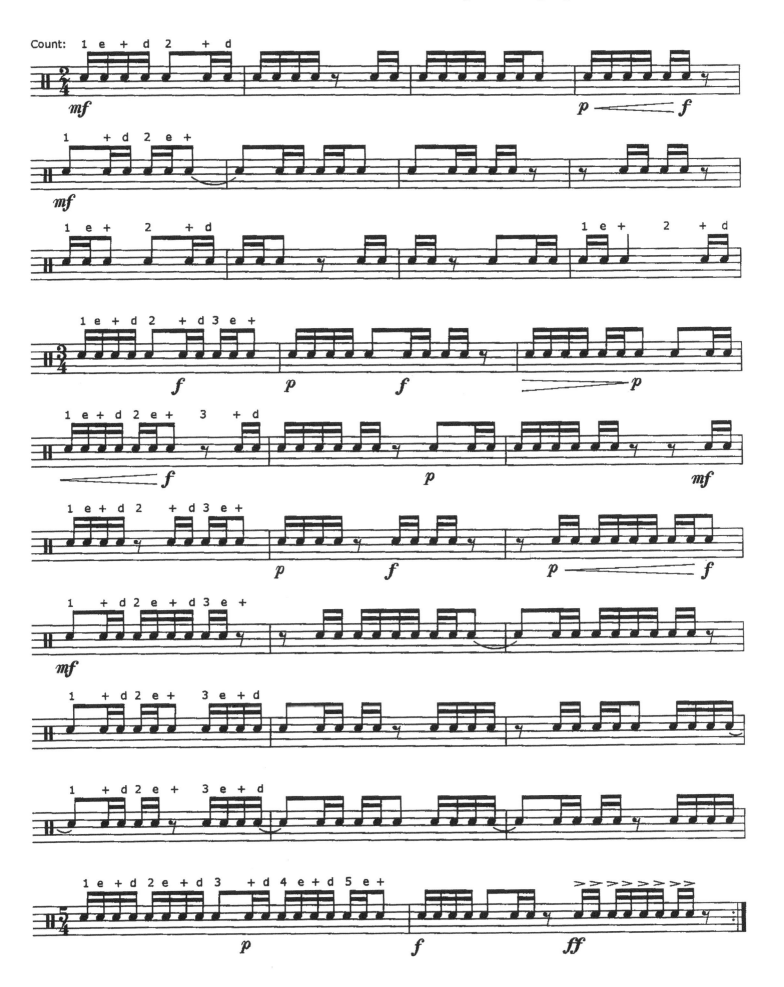

READING (♪♫♫) (♪ ♫) (♫)
WITH THE BASS DRUM INCLUDED

MORE READING WITH BASS DRUM INCLUDED

INTRODUCING 16TH NOTE RESTS (𝄿)

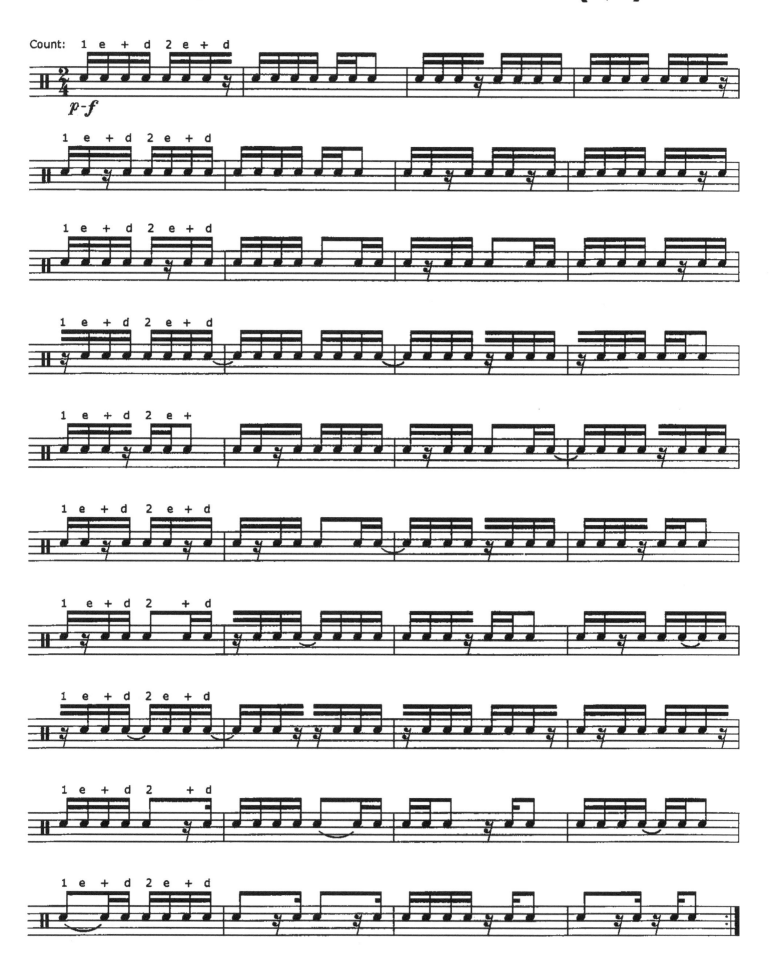

READING 16TH RESTS CONTINUED

INTRODUCING DOTTED 8ᵀᴴ NOTES

An eighth-note has the value of two sixteenth notes. Since a dot placed after a note increases its duration by half, than a dotted eighth-note has the value of three sixteenth-notes, needing a 16th-note or 16th-rest to complete one full beat in "quarter-time."

INTRODUCING DOUBLE DOTS AFTER 1/2 AND 1/4 NOTES

A single dot placed after a note increases its duration by half more its original value. Two dots placed after a note increases its duration by three fourths.

PART FOUR

READING SYNCOPATED RHYTHMS WITH 8TH AND 16TH NOTES

While eighth-notes usually fall on the downbeat or upbeat (the counts of "1" or "an"), in reading syncopated rhythmic patterns with eighth and sixteenth notes, the eight-note appears on the count "e," with the subsequent shift of a natural accent to the count of "e."

There are six basic syncopated rhythmic patterns with eighth and sixteenth-notes:

BASIC SYNCOPATED PATTERN NUMBER 1

BASIC SYNCOPATED PATTERN NUMBER 2

BASIC SYNCOPATED PATTERN NUMBERS 3 & 4

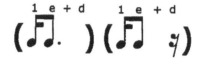

BASIC SYNCOPATED PATTERN NUMBERS 5 & 6

READING 8TH & 16TH SYNCOPATION
WITH BASS DRUM INCLUDED

READING COMBINATIONS OF
1/4, 1/8, & 1/16 NOTE SYNCOPATION

PART FIVE

READING SYNCOPATED RHYTHMS WITH 8TH & 16TH NOTE TRIPLETS

A triplet is a group of three notes played in the time of two notes of the same value.

According to part of the definition, syncopation in 4/4 time occurs if the stress is not on the first and third beat. Therefore, stressing any part of the triplet other than the downbeats of one and three produces the sound of syncopated triplets. Most, but not all, of the exercises on the following pages will produce a syncopated triplet sound.

There are several ways to count eighth-note triplets, but I suggest counting with the sound of "ta" as in the word "tap."

If you want to read with speed, eventually you will have to count with just downbeats and "feel" the other two notes of 8th triplets.

INTRODUCING 8TH TRIPLETS (♪♫♪)

8TH TRIPLETS AND 8TH NOTES

Note: The last line shows 8th triplets combined with 16th-notes.

8TH TRIPLETS WITH A REST IN THE MIDDLE (JAZZ FEEL)

Note: I suggest you count the full 8th triplet (♪♪♪) with just a downbeat, and "feel" the following two notes. Also, try using the sticking RRL on a full triplet (♪♪♪).

INTRODUCING A REST ON THE UPBEAT TRIPLET (♪♪ 𝄾)

INTRODUCING A REST ON THE DOWNBEAT TRIPLET (𝄾 ♪♪)

INTRODUCING TWO RESTS ON 8TH TRIPLETS

READING 8TH TRIPLETS IN SPACE

READING 8TH TRIPLETS WITH BASS DRUM INCLUDED

INTRODUCING 1/4 NOTE TRIPLETS

INTRODUCING 1/2 NOTE TRIPLETS

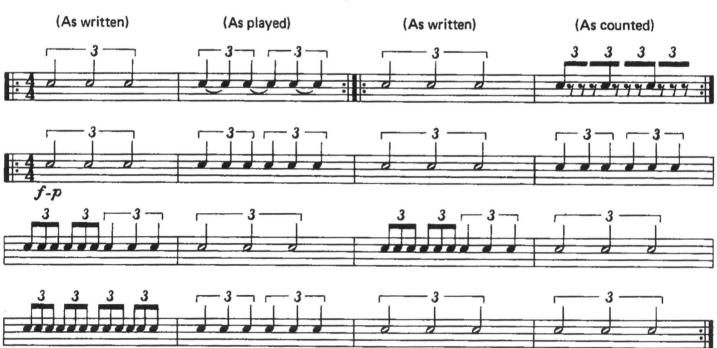

INTRODUCING 16TH TRIPLETS FROM THE UPBEAT (♩ ♫)

Note: If you want to read with speed, drop the "ta ta" part of the count and simply say 1 + 2 +.

16TH TRIPLETS FROM THE DOWNBEAT

16TH TRIPLETS ON THE UPBEAT AND DOWNBEAT

PART SIX

MEASURED
DOUBLE-STROKE ROLLS
ON SYNCOPATED RHYTHMS

Before presenting reading exercises with measured rolls on syncopated rhythms, the first two pages in this section will present preparatory exercises with measured rolls on 1/2, 1/4, and 1/8-note rhythms which are not necessarily syncopated. Subsequent pages will then present an extensive array of measured double-stroke rolls on syncopated rhythms.

IMPORTANT: After playing the exercises as written with measured double-strokes, try replaying the rolls using single-strokes.

MEASURED ROLLS ON TIED 1/4 & 1/2 NOTES
(9 STROKES TO THE 1/4 NOTE ROLL)

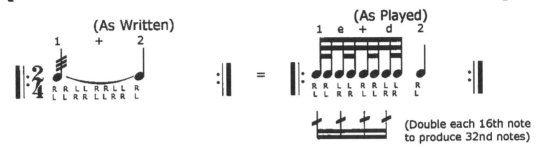

IMPORTANT: End a roll on the note it is tied to. A 9-stroke roll includes 8 strokes — the note it ends on constitutes the 9th stroke.

INTRODUCING MEASURED 5-STROKE ROLLS

TIED 1/8 NOTE ROLLS FROM THE DOWNBEAT

TIED 1/8 NOTE ROLLS FROM THE UPBEAT

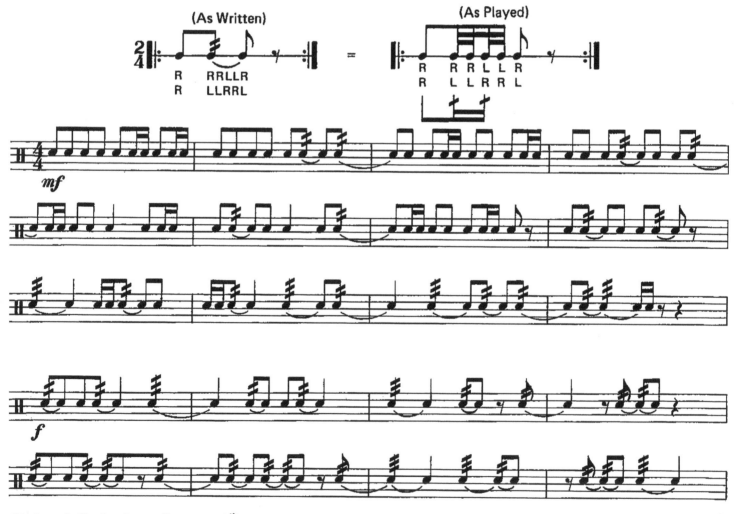

Note: A 5-stroke roll to an 8th note includes 4 strokes — the note it ends on constitutes the 5th stroke.

MEASURED ROLLS ON SYNCOPATED RHYTHMS

(continue rolling)

INTRODUCING

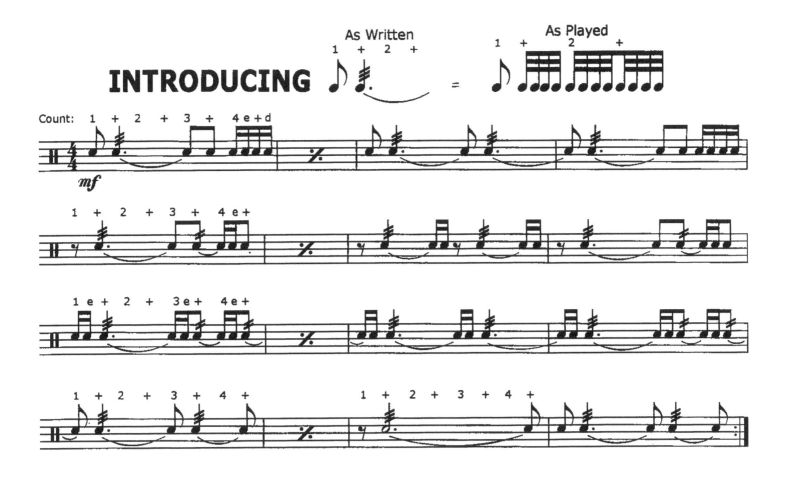

MEASURED ROLLS ON SYNCOPATED RHYTHMS OVER 3 BEATS IN 3/4 TIME

INTRODUCING MEASURED ROLLS WITHOUT TIES
ON SYNCOPATED RHYTHMS

At moderate to fast tempos rolls without ties must end just before the next beat as shown in the following examples:

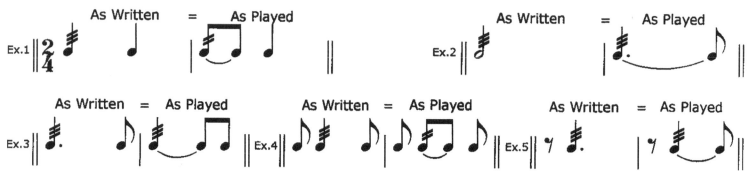

Note: Numbers above the rolls indicate the number of strokes in that roll.

MEASURED ROLLS ON 8TH & 16TH NOTE SYNCOPATED RHYTHMS
INTRODUCING THE TIED "INSIDE" 5-STROKE ROLL

INTRODUCING THE 7-STROKE ROLL ON SYNCOPATED RHYTHMS
TIED DOTTED 8TH NOTE ROLLS FROM THE DOWNBEAT

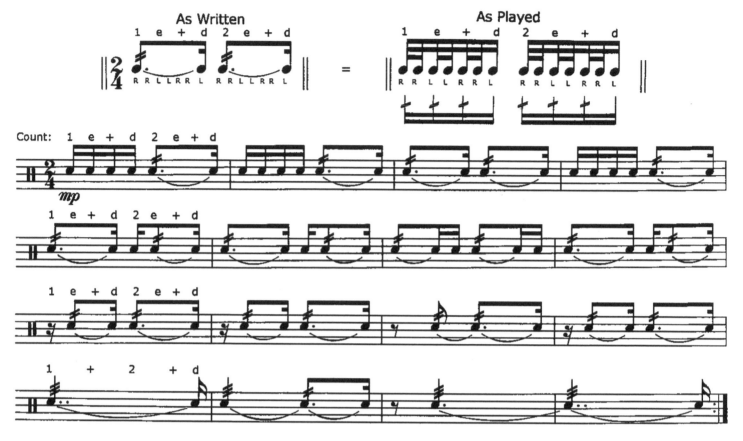

TIED DOTTED 8TH NOTE ROLLS FROM THE COUNT OF "E"

Note: The 7-stroke roll includes 6 strokes — the note it ends on constitutes the 7th stroke.

SUMMARY OF MEASURED ROLLS FROM 1/2, 1/4, 1/8, & 1/16 NOTES
ON SYNCOPATED RHYTHMS

PART SEVEN

ACCENT PATTERNS WITH 8ᵀᴴ NOTES AND 8ᵀᴴ TRIPLETS PRODUCING SYNCOPATED SOUNDS

The pages in this section are taken directly from my book, **ACCENTS AND SOLOS FOR ROCK AND JAZZ DRUMMING.** Exercises are presented with accents both on and off the beat. When notes are accented off the beat they produce a very syncopated sound. Try to develop two and four-bar solos based upon the exercises on the next few pages. All exercises are shown with alternating sticking, leading with the right hand.

Other ways of practicing the exercises are as follows:

1) Play all exercises with the right hand alone, the left hand alone, or alternating sticks leading with the left hand.

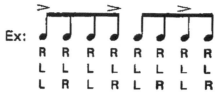

2) Replay the exercises and flam all accented notes using the notated sticking as well as the three suggested stickings.

(Note: You could also try playing drags and ruffs on accented notes).

3) Replay all 8ᵗʰ note exercises and interpret them with a jazz triplet feel.

4) Place all accented notes on a tom tom, and all unaccented notes on the snare drum.

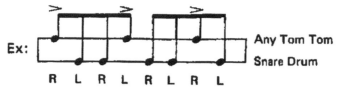

5) Place all accented notes on a tom tom, but this time play the unaccented notes with double strokes. This effectively changes each eighth note into two sixteenth notes.

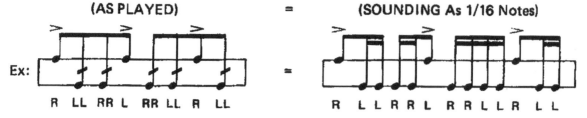

Note: Although no bass drum part is written play your bass on every beat, or on one and three. You can also try playing your bass together with accented notes.

INTRODUCING ACCENTED 8TH NOTES IN 4/4 TIME FOR ONE BAR

DOWNBEAT ACCENTS

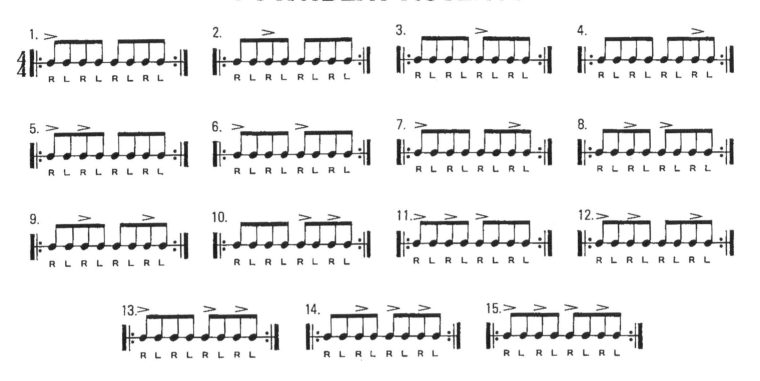

UPBEAT ACCENTS

DOWNBEAT AND UPBEAT ACCENTS

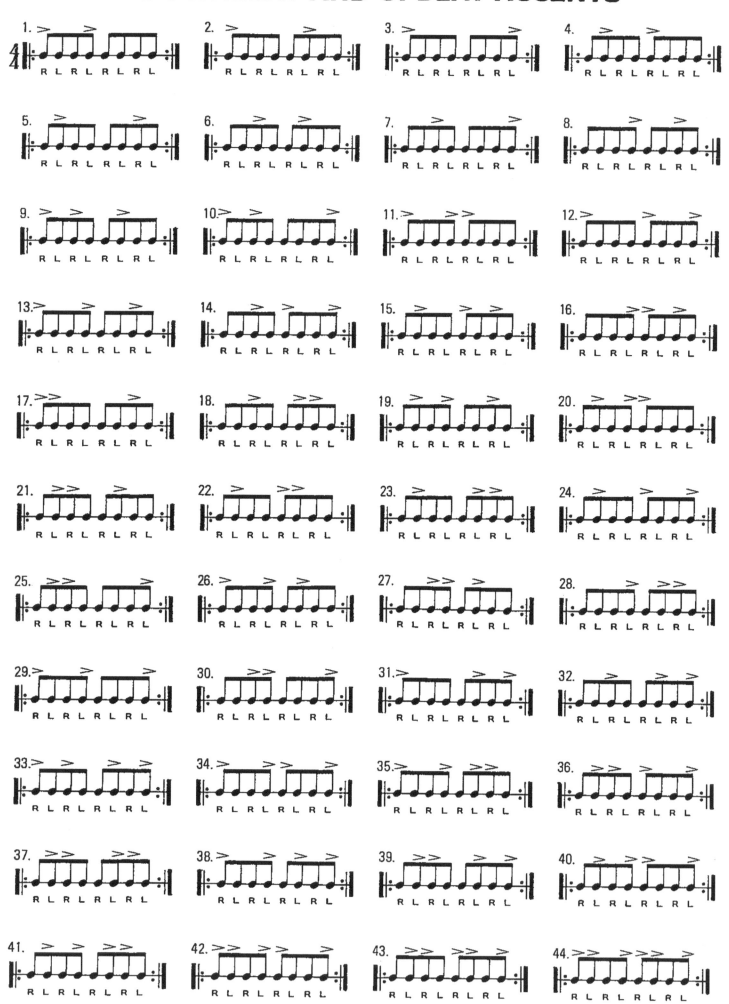

ACCENTS ON 8TH NOTES FOR TWO BARS

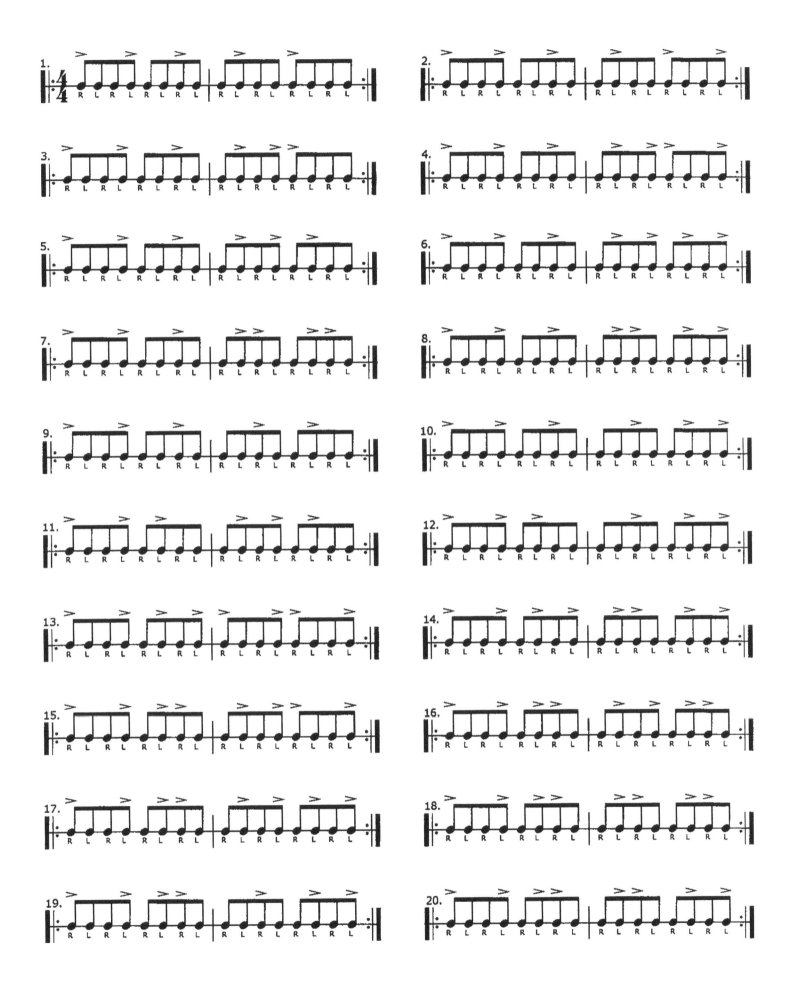

ACCENTS ON 8TH NOTES FOR TWO BARS CONTINUED

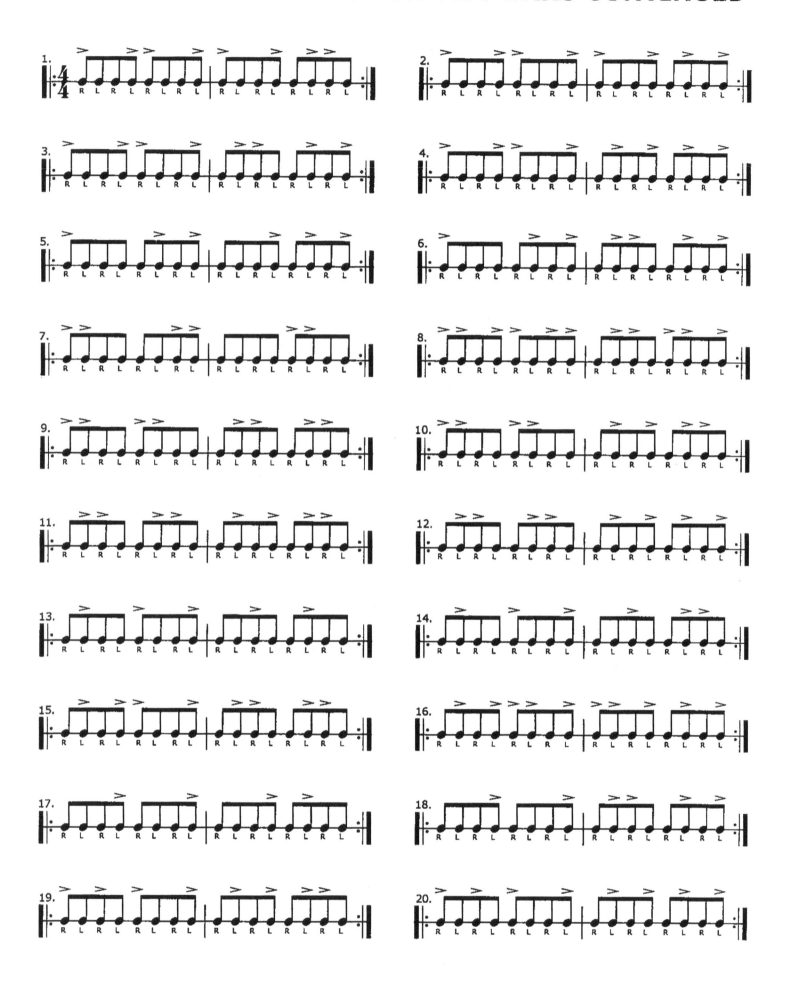

ACCENTS ON 8TH NOTES
IN 3/4 AND 5/4 TIME
FOR ONE AND TWO BARS

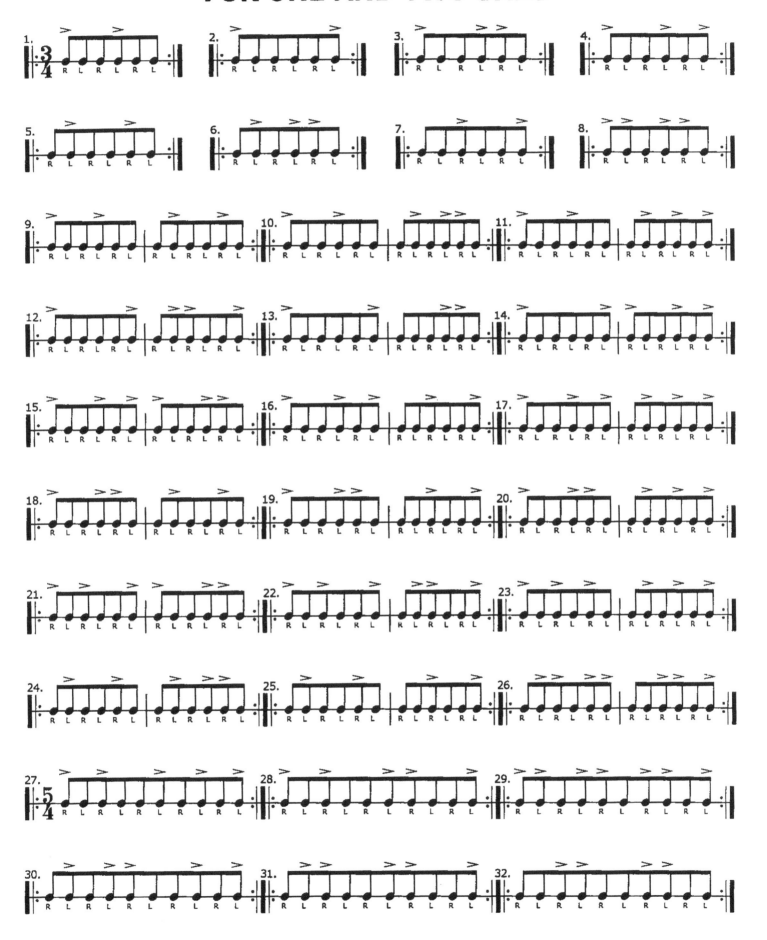

INTRODUCING ACCENTED 8TH NOTE TRIPLETS

DOWNBEAT ACCENTS

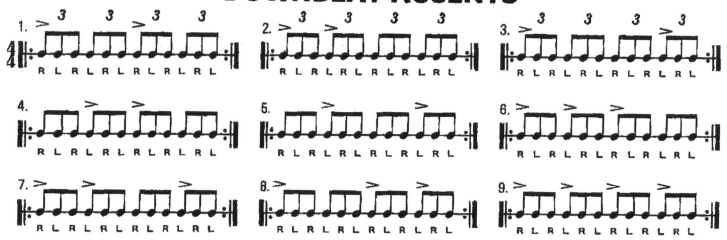

UPBEAT ACCENTS

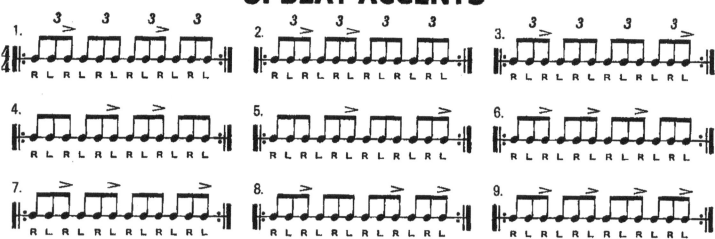

DOWNBEAT AND UPBEAT ACCENTS

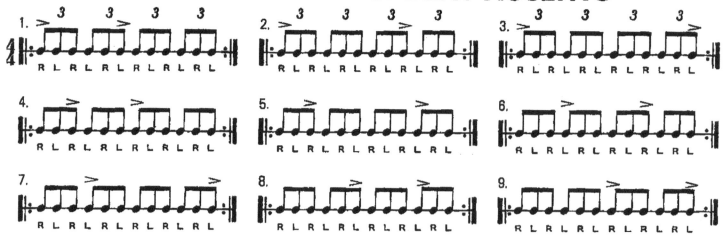

In order to avoid cluttering the page the number "3" is only placed over the groups of triplets in the first three exercises

DOWNBEAT AND UPBEAT ACCENTS (Continued)

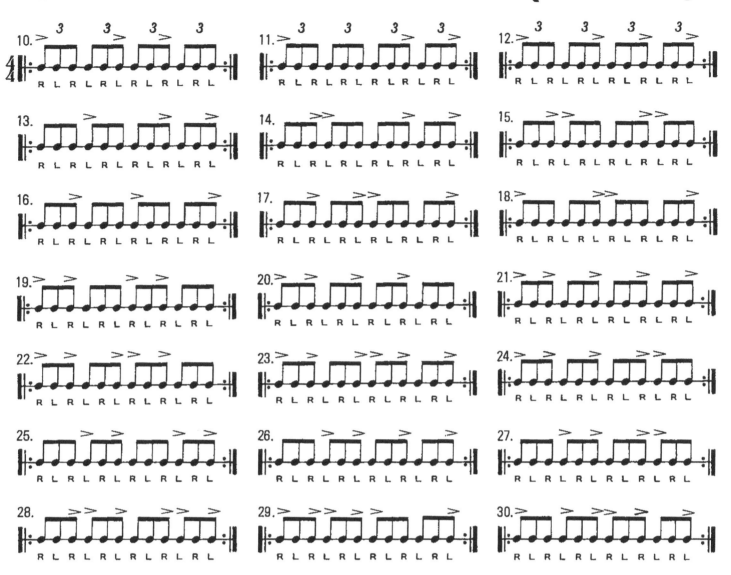

MIDDLE TRIPLET ACCENTS

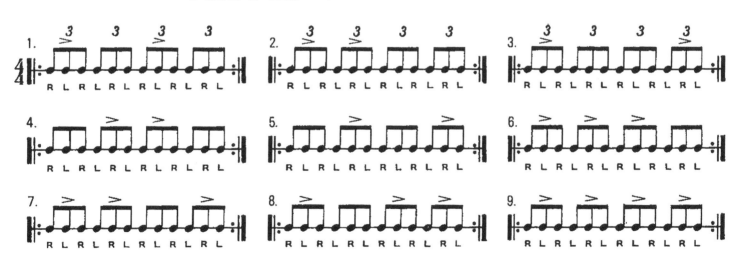

DOWNBEAT AND MIDDLE TRIPLET ACCENTS

DOWNBEAT, UPBEAT AND MIDDLE TRIPLET ACCENTS

PART EIGHT

STICKING PATTERNS
FOR
SYNCOPATED SOUNDS
WITH
8TH NOTES
THEN
8TH TRIPLETS

The sticking patterns on the following pages, when played up to speed, produce natural accents with syncopated sounds. Although the right/left sticking is notated on just one leger line, I suggest you divide the rhythm by playing the right hand part between the tom toms, while the left hand part remains on the snare.

BASIC STICKING PATTERNS
FOR SYNCOPATED SOUNDS
WITH 8TH-NOTES FOR ONE BAR

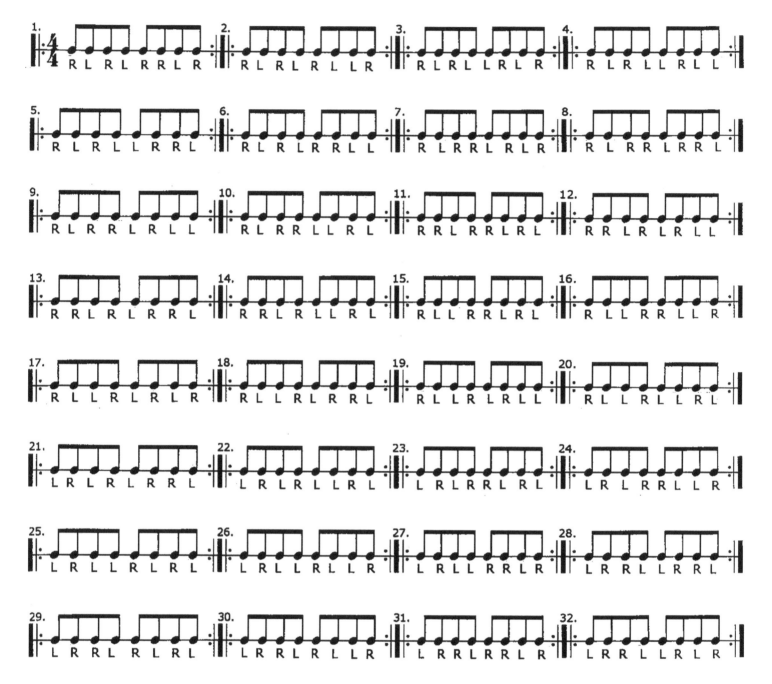

IMPORTANT: In order to bring out the syncopated sound of each sticking pattern try singing the right-hand part with any one-syllable sound such as "di" as in the word "did," and play the left hand part more or less as ghost notes.

After playing the exercises as indicated, replay each one and sing the left-hand part, while playing the right-hand part more or less as ghost notes.

COMBINING 8TH NOTE STICKING PATTERNS FOR TWO BARS

GROUP 1

Note: In each group the first bar contains the same sticking pattern, while the sticking pattern changes in the second bar.

GROUP 2

GROUP 3

GROUP 4

GROUP 5

GROUP 6

GROUP 7

GROUP 8

84

GROUP 9

GROUP 10

GROUP 11

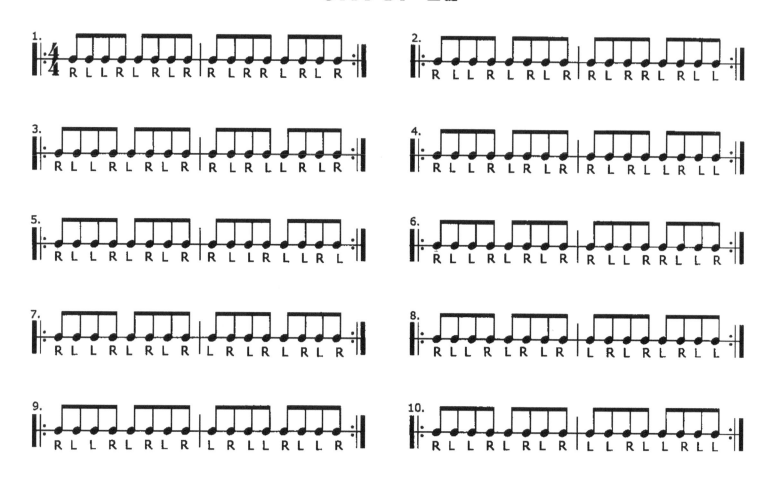

GROUP 12

GROUP 13

GROUP 14

8TH NOTE STICKING PATTERNS FOR FOUR BARS

Note: Each four-bar exercise is written in the AABA form, meaning the 1st, 2nd, and 4th bars are the same — it's only in the 3rd bar that the sticking pattern changes.

STICKING PATTERNS FOR SYNCOPATED SOUNDS WITH 8TH NOTES IN 3/4 TIME, THEN 5/4 TIME

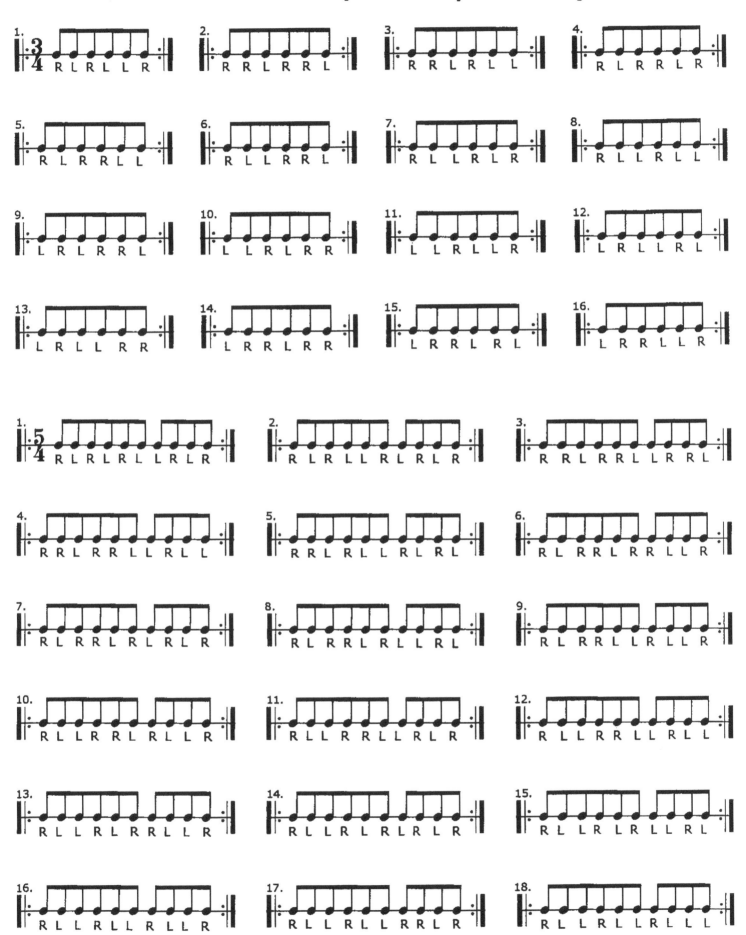

STICKING PATTERNS FOR SYNCOPATED SOUNDS
WITH 8TH TRIPLETS

BASIC STICKING PATTERNS

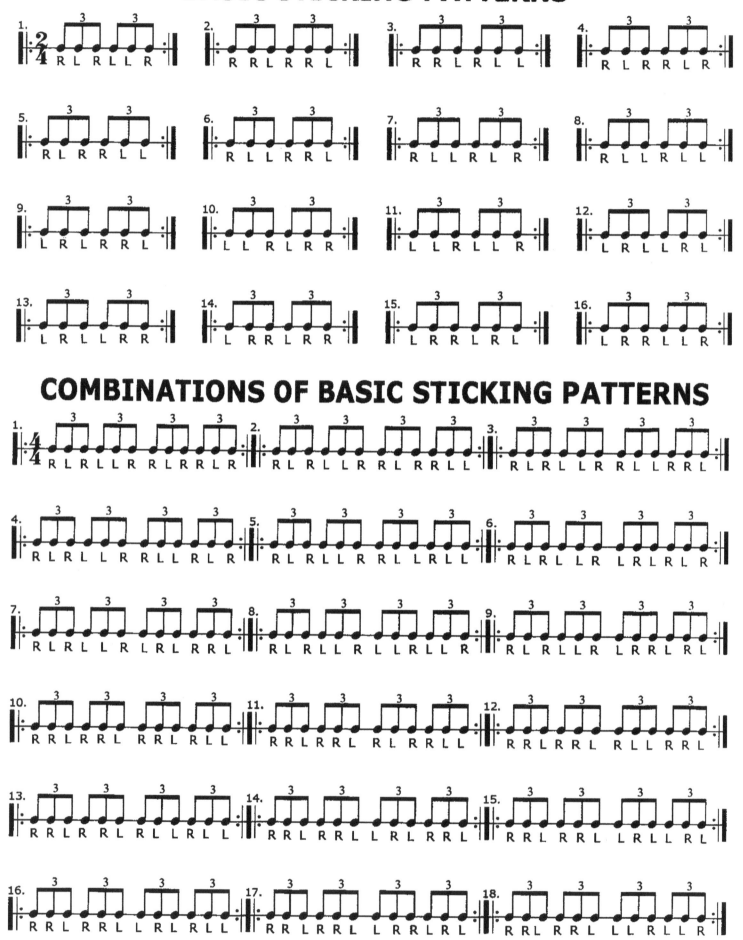

COMBINATIONS OF BASIC STICKING PATTERNS
CONTINUED

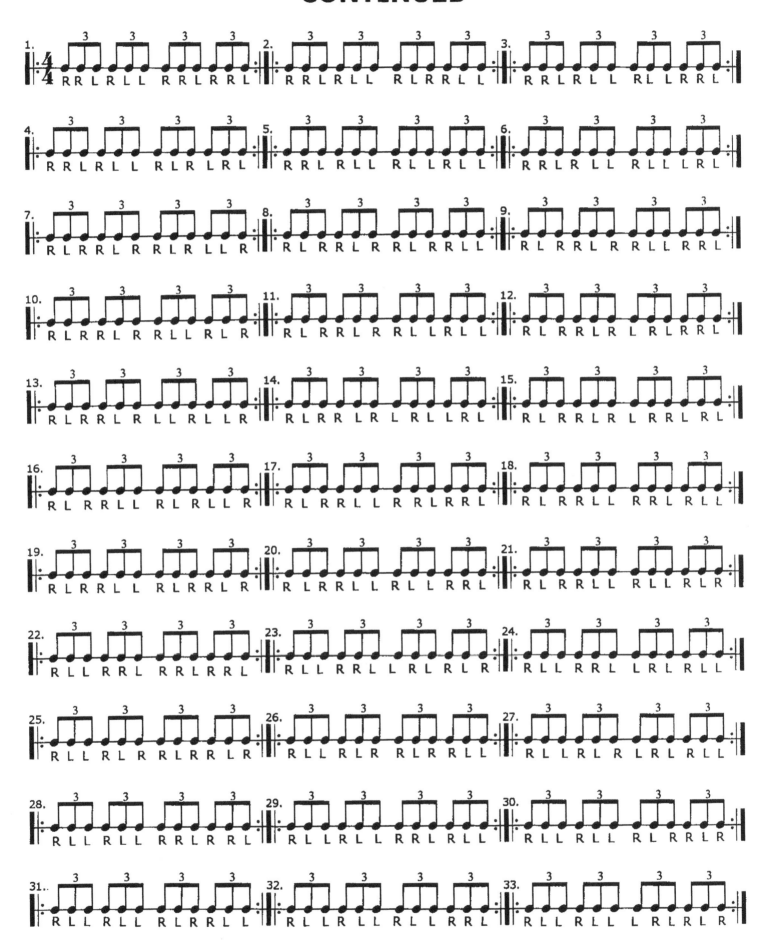

STICKING PATTERNS WITH 8TH TRIPLETS FOR FOUR BARS